LETTERS TO MY SONS

REFLECTIONS OF A FATHER

DARRYL PORTER

authorHOUSE®

AuthorHouse™
1663 Liberty Drive
Bloomington, IN 47403
www.authorhouse.com
Phone: 833-262-8899

Published by AuthorHouse 10/27/2020

ISBN: 978-1-6655-0547-5 (sc)
ISBN: 978-1-6655-0546-8 (e)

Library of Congress Control Number: 2020920976

Acknowledgements and Dedication

First, I would like to thank my God, who is the God of Abraham, the God of Isaac, the God of Israel, for giving me the greatest gift of all, Life. I would love to thank him for leading me through the passageway of ignorance and darkness into the hallway of brightness and wisdom, and for bestowing upon me the power of understanding which are the gifts of the Prophets. I thank the family I am blessed with for their patience, support and constant love. Peace and love to my mother and father (deceased) true soldiers! Thanks to all my aunts and uncles for your examples. To the love of my life. To Dell II, Shaina, Malik, Jeremiah and Dominique You all are the reason I do what I do. To Dell III, Sincere, Anya and Zoey Pop-Pop loves you. To the Red and White – MAB4LIFE- "WHO YOU WIT!".

To all the teachers who put up with me and had the patience to give me skills to be the best I can be. Last yet surely not the least this book is dedicated to the men who taught, guided and showed me what a man does. And the boys who helped me be a man and who are now are men themselves.

23Feb16

As I grow older age wise my mental & spiritual fortitude has also grown. I am no longer the angry young man world at the world for no reason, to an aging spiritually led man. The problem with this is that in today's society that's something that's not popular. The real issue is this was the way society used to be but society has gotten away from that because being led by "strong spiritually based men" isn't good for masses any longer. It is a threat to the structural & monetary based society we live in. Yet the same book that most use to take vows of marriage, oath for an elected office & being on the witness stand shows that from the beginning we were led by strong spiritually based men. Men who kept the whole duty of man. Which you will find in Ecclesiastes chapter 12 verse 13. But they forgot this at some point and allowed themselves to be enslaved. The bad thing is that society today still has the same thought pattern which is sad. We refuse to see that this is the reason we are in the condition we are in; in the neighborhood, community, city, states & world we live in. The errors of our men derive from the demeanor of our ancestors. Examples of this can be found in the Bible in the book of Genesis throughout the entire book. In the beginning of the Bible man was commanded by the Creator to obey His commands but man didn't and was hard headed like my sons. Something that I as your dad has also experienced. As I get older sons I realize that as a youth I too lost that sense of direction, the respect of my elders, understanding my responsibility & listening to my father. At times see in society it is and has become OK to not have, to listen to, and/or respect your father. Something that is crazy because from a spiritual point we pray the Lord's Prayer and it starts out by saying "Our Father" yet the respect of fathers is shoved upon in our society, neighborhoods, communities, cities and states. The issue is that our forefathers passed down wrong from generation to generation because they allowed crafty council to be taken upon themselves by not obeying the Creator my sons. It's very important that you grasp, understand and know this. To understand what I am talking about will take time and effort of doing things such as reading and researching what information is presented to you. Reading more positive thinking books, and last yet not least reading, asking and studying the Bible more. This will help you understand me better than before. This will also help you grow as a man, a person, a husband yet most of all my son a child of the Creator. So at this may thee Creator bless you & keep you. Lift up his face to shine & give you peace!!!

Good Night

I HAVE SEEN DAYS WHERE THE COLOR OF MY SKIN AFFECTED people in manners that caused them to hate me yet the hatred that hurts me the most was the hate I accustomed from those who looked just like me. This has always baffled me until I came to know myself. Until I humbled myself I had very little peace in my life. I had to change my thought patterns to become more open minded, allow for the Creator to use me in a way to help others by my actions and stop having so much hate towards self. The hard part is that it's not popular in our communities, cities, schools, states & even churches to have knowledge of self. We are programmed to beat down everything about self that's positive so that we stay in that place of being controlled & self hatred. It's so sad that we think so less of ourselves but the truth of the matter is that it's our own fault that we continue to live in this state cause we're afraid of change, don't think it's so bad anymore or just damn right don't care. We continue to exhibit the same slave mentality as our ancestors did cause we forgot where we came from and who we are. We are taught that we are inferior to the masses, that we are a "minority" but how can we be a minority when the Creator promised that our "seeds" shall be like the grains of sand until the end of time. This is a covenant the Creator made with our forefathers yet this isn't something that you are told on a daily basis which is why you don't know it or think this way. It would cause so much damage to the structure of society if you knew this and/or was taught that you are important, have values, came from royalty and are the beginning of this world. See to stay in control they teach that you are a "minority" so they can project that they are the majority when actually they are the minority. Some fear that they are not able to be in control so that is the reason to tell these lies. We also help this happen by thinking less of each other, putting each other down, killing each other, stealing from each other but most of all we disrespect self. Lest we start to think of self as being important, of values, kings of our castles, leaders in our neighborhoods the same cycles of destruction will plague our people. If we don't change the slave mentality that most have we will remain and always be a "minority" because of our thoughts, ways & actions. Your existence will be that of a slave which was taught they were the "minority" so the slavemaster could impose his control. See the way you think leads you to the way you live. If you think inferior you will live inferior. My sons in life the Creator gives you choices. The choice to live as only he can or the choice to be enslaved in your own thoughts. The Creator made you in His image and called you His child which makes you a prince, royalty, leader of people, father of many nations and most of all you're not a "minority" never was never will be; only in thought if we don't change mentally soon as possible. They took the shackles off our feet and put them on our minds. So may the Creator bless you & keep you & lift up His face to shine & give you peace.

GN

28Feb16

"*As* I get older I no longer listen to what to what men say I watch what they do." Andrew Carnige. This is a quote that I heard watching a TV show. It stuck with me cause it makes sense. It's basically saying that it's not what you say it's about what you do. This also is how the creator judges man. According to scripture God judges man based on his "deeds". Deeds means actions/what you do. Today's society is about a lot of talking people saying a lot and doing nothing. It's not that hard to understand why this happens; it's simply man hasn't "done" what the Creator has said from the beginning. Yet man does a lot of talking about nothing. Man doesn't "do" the will of the Creator because it's not what is popular/hip/cool. Our ancestors have been avoiding their responsibilities for some time now and because they acted in the manner they did we suffer today. Our ancestors have run and lied through their own journey so long that their irresponsible ways have affected the mentality of our people still today. What we need to do is to understand that change only comes when you "do" something. Talk is cheap. If your actions don't match what you say then your

words become lies. See in life it's not about what you say it's about what you "do." We as people have gotten so far away from the creator that most don't know, think about, or acknowledge the creator and his great presence that is in all of our lives yet we don't acknowledge it. We are taught by our parents who were taught by their parents who were taught by their parents which may have been slaves. Hence the slave mentality of the generations throughout our homes, neighborhoods, communities, cities, states & nation. To change the ways of our people IT must start at home meaning with yourself. To change the way we live it starts with self first, then acknowledge God, then self, family, friends and become responsible for your own actions. We have been people of saying a lot but doing nothing which is why we suffer today. The sad part is that talking gets in the way of progress cause we get stuck on what's being said instead of understanding what's being said then doing it. Here's the thing we listen to what is being said, not always hearing what is said and definitely not understanding what is being said. Then we go out in the world filled with unless information because we don't truly hear, listen and/or understand the lessons we are taught because we are programmed to talk a lot, not listen, don't hear and for sure try hard not to understand anything positive, good, and/or about self/the Creator. We aren't taught that learning, knowing and thinking about the Creator is learning about self. If you knew this you wouldn't have the slave mentality that society wants, needs you to have so that the masses can be controlled by the "few". So may the Creator bless you & keep you lifting up his face to shine & give you peace.

Bless You

7Jul16

As I write today it's with so much anger. I've lived my life as a God fearing, loving, responsible individual and yet I had to be subjected to the racial ills of the American way. I was assaulted by a Phila. Police officer who felt he had rights over me. And once he felt he had no control over me he resorted to the only recourse he had at the time which was to beat on me. I had always been taught to respect the police yet in my community the respect of police isn't what they reflect towards the community. It has caused me to view how we as a group are looked upon. It will make you look at history. His "story" is always filled with violence, control, taking and elimination. They have been violent from the time they came to this land which was already occupied. We as the investors have been here numerous times doing business with the inhabitants of this land numerous times prior to Columbus coming here. These are the descendants of slave masters so their actions are "expected" all we have to do is look at his ways and actions from the beginning of time. His ways have always been opposite of ours we love, care and respect. He lies, kills and destroys. And now we have inherited these

7

ways. We do these things to each other without thoughts doing the deeds of the slave masters to/for each other. Then when he does these things to us we want to scream out the sad thing is we don't scream out when we do it. To ourselves. Don't get me wrong I don't agree with the way we are treated by them yet to be treated better it must start within. If you start respecting yourself first you can get others to respect you. We have forgotten that we are children of the Creator, we have followed the ways/deeds of others for so long we don't know who we are. We have a tendency to want to belong to everything/anything except belonging to self. We don't reflect on ourselves; we tend to blame instead of "doing something" to make a change. Some of it comes from wanting to be "accepted". The truth of the matter is that man can't give you rights the Creator gives you rights and him only. What has to be remembered is the Creator chose us to be his children so if we remember that and do his will we will be alright. Yet that is the main issue in our community we have forgotten and until we remember & do these ills we suffer will continue cause it's "our history" we were slaves in Egypt for four hundred plus years & slaves for four hundred plus years here yet we don't see the parity. So my sons don't let the cars, jewelry, houses & money fool you. We will always be inferior in the eyes of the slave masters & his descendants yet the creator didn't make you inferior to anyone so keep your head up pray often and ask for strength to fight a good battle in this war called life based on the world we live in.

Peace & Blessings

I'M WRITING TO YOU TODAY OUT OF REFLECTION OF MY LIFE experiences and the things that are happening around me in society. Today some 53 years after my existence the same attitude towards my culture then has reared its ugly head. The lives of men of color doesn't matter and those of the opposite race continue their assault on our men with the fear of their presence. Back then they hid behind white hoods nowadays they hide in the uniforms of the police departments across this country. Just like now as in my youth they marched, protested and stood ground together. Yet when they were given the opportunity to own things some attitudes changed and some began to hate themselves because of economics, finances and things. So the separation began and to make it even more successful they put us in projects: Close living quarters with very minimal commodities. So the plan of elimination was set and we have helped by doing exactly what they want and need us to do to help keep them in control. We must become lawful men again. We have stepped so far away from self that we are still mentally stuck in slave mentality. We tend to act like we don't remember that those in control of today's society are the 3rd & 4th generations descendants of the slave master's. See their fears are being broke, not reproducing, that as a culture we are growing financially, economically, and definitely spiritually. The problem is that we are growing the way they want us to grow learning of a deity that looks like them. What we don't realize is that when you're taught that the creator doesn't look like you and looks like the same individual that's suppressing you, killing you, raping you, degrading you and most of all use you for his gains not yours. We have adapted his mannerisms so much that we hate self as much as he does. It's so troubling how we don't respect, love and/ or appreciate each other so how will others do those things towards us. Until we demand respect within self we will be disrespected by others. Until we change the way we think we will be in the position we are in. We can't look for others to give us anything, especially respect for ourselves. We have to remember and understand that we set the tone of how we will be treated. My son the learning and understanding of love, respect and appreciation starts at home. We must remember that we are the children of the Creator and according to his holy words we are the princes, priests and leaders of this world the only problem is that we don't know this. Once the change in mentality starts then our actions will change and the respect of self will begin and then maybe others will respect us. So my sons it is very important that you remember to maintain self-respect, pray often, ask the Creator to strengthen you where you may be weak, build a hedge around you for anyone to keep from doing you any hurt harm or danger and always be conscience that there are those that will hate you for being you. Be aware at all times we are at war. So may the Creator keep you and lift up his face to shine and give you peace. Bless You

GN

22 July 16

ODAY IS GOING TO BE THE HOTTEST OF THE YEAR AND IN the neighborhoods the tendencies of violence are lurking. Preying on the youth of today like a vulture over a carcass. Yet the youth of today doesn't understand that praying can keep & help them from being prey. The predators have laid down so many traps for our people in general that the assistance from our youth with the constant killing of one another makes their quest easier. To maintain dominance over our people they project this image of superiority to make us believe/feel they are the majority until we think. The world is made of more places with people of color as the majority of the population so how could they be the majority. If you allow yourself to be fooled mentally by accepting the bilking that has been placed on so many then you will just be one of the masses also subjected to the foolishness. To stop the constant downward spiral that has plagued our people for centuries; because generations of accepting responsibility for not doing right wasn't taught we first must regroup as a people before we can get others to start to respect us. To get others to start treating us as we should we must first treat each other with the same respect we want for self. See our living conditions are the constant wanting of things has us so frustrated that the instant someone says or does something minor it can turn into a very vital situation. This self hate is the real reason that others treat us in the manner they do. How can someone respect the wishes of us being respected by them when we don't respect each other. That's ridiculous. Until we stop the senseless killing of each other how can we complain about the cops killing men of color at an alarming rate. Yes the killing of men of color by the cops/legal authorities is very wrong yet not something that's new in this country. It's happened before when the machine felt threatened by the demands of a people suppressed by their establishment. See the hatred of us as a people still exists today as it has since the Creator led us out of Egypt. Yet the biggest and most hurtful assault on our people is the deserted amongst ourselves. We hate ourselves more than the enemy. We hate one another because of skin tone, things, money, lack of respect. And just about every small matter. So to get better it has to start at home. We need men to be men. Teaching their experiences so they could be examples to the next generations to follow. We need to be more reflective of the past not only your own experiences but those of your forefathers. The rise and fall of something starts with its people, their values, their goals, their dedication and definitely their responsibilities. If they forget and/or neglect any parts of one of these they are subjected to be fooled, amused, embarrassed, controlled, enslaved. So my sons may you always think, stay true to yourself, be one with the Creator, love family, friends and also remember that others view you differently no matter whether they look like you or they don't. Again as I leave you prayer can/will keep you from being prey. So let the words of your mouth and the meditations of your heart be acceptable in thine sight and know whence your help comes from. These will definitely keep you through your life and aid you in times of trouble.

Peace & Blessings

*T*HE JOURNEY OF LIFE IS ONE OF MANY LAYERS WE START OUT an egg that develops into a fetus which becomes a baby as the baby grows into a toddler then a child growing into a teen then an adult all this represents constant change which is consistently with the creator we grow as individuals as the earth grows in its seasons, that the creator made for us to have as an example of constant growth. We don't think about the parities of life cause we're not taught to relate to the creator in our daily life yet the importance of having the knowledge, understanding and acceptance of the creator in our lives is essential. Change is what happens daily yet it's what most of us don't like. Change means to do something and most don't want to do anything. Change is essential in life yet it scares most individuals cause we become creatures of our environment. It's what helps mold us as individuals. What we fail to acknowledge is that change is inevitable; it's part of our lives from conception. Yet we tend to have a hard time with the changes of life. It's constant you go from someone doing everything for you to trying your best to do for yourself. Change is all around us yet it's not always grasped in a manner that's best suited for our living condition. For example we as a people were brought to a land that wasn't conducive to how we lived. We were made slaves. A situation that we weren't accustomed to. Yet that's not foreign to our people. We were slaves before cause we refused to change our wayward ways. The lack of change is the reason that our people continue to be in the plight we are in. We refuse to change the way we think, the way we do things, the way we allow others to think and/or treat us. The way we treat each other must change first before we change others to change the way they treat us. Changing the thought patterns is what will change the way we're treated. Yet again it's something that takes work, doing something, making a conscious effort to change. The problem with that is change makes those that are in control uncomfortable. See with change it means that the masses will have to become responsible for their actions. They will have to change their mentality first. They have to start to relate to the creator and self. If this happens then they can start to make changes towards the way they treat/think of self. If this happens then the effort of getting others to treat our people like they should be treated will possibly be possible. And if it's possible we must continue to grow mentally which sometimes is the hardest thing to do. Life has so many obstacles/distractions that staying focused mentally is hard at times yet not impossible. And growing mentally will/is (a) constant change. So my son, the grasp of change as early as possible will allow your journey in life to be as less stressful as it can be. Growth and change will allow you to deal with life's tribulations. Stay focused, be aware at all times, control what you can control, change what you have the ability to change, respect self as well as others, remain healthy and most of all love. Love is the key to change. Love yourself and you can change so much. Cause you can't love anyone else until you love self & the Creator first and remember this is the key to change. So let the words of your mouth and the meditations of your heart be acceptable in thine sight and know when your help comes from. Cause you are the light of change & the true light of the world.

Peace & Blessings

ODAY I SPOKE TO A FEMALE ACQUAINTANCE WHOM I HADN'T spoken to in some time and during our conversation she mentioned how males today aren't about love. She said that her experiences are that they don't pay attention and lack communication skills. I sat and listened as she offered her thoughts on the matter and when she finished I offered my thoughts. First I started by going to the heart of the issue: The home life of each one of us. It was a time where most households had both parents and the family structure was set by the grounds of men being the head of the household and the women ran the home. Children were taught the meaning of love through the eyes of their parents based upon what they saw and/or heard. If our parents grew up with both mom and dad it was likely they would exhibit the same actions cause it was what they saw and was taught. It was exhibited in the music they heard, the few TV shows they were allowed to watch (if they had a TV), school and especially in the church. Young men were taught to be respectful of females, cherish them, treat them as they would treat their moms or grandmoms. It was taboo to date without having the blessings of the female parents when trying to court her. And it was definite that if you wanted to get married you went to her father and asked his permission to marry his daughter. Now don't get me wrong there were incidents of teenage pregnancies but they were few and handled differently from today cause of the embarrassment the family felt when a teenage pregnancy concurred. Because the family structure was devastated over the course of time and sex replaced love in relationships between males and females, hence the state of today's heavy dosage of failed marriages, single parent homes, multiple children fathered by different men, deadbeat parents, grandparents raising children and most of all the acceptance of wrong. We accept so much wrong where relationships are concerned that the important parts of what a male/female relationship should be becomes overlooked or just not paid any attention because the ills of what society says is acceptable in a relationship. Start with a foundation, like having goals that are alike, being able to give support at her best & worst moments, being able to sit and listen when she's upset or just venting. Tell her she's beautiful just because, remember when she's there at your worst moment don't ever forget she's a queen, she's soft as pure gold, hard as steel, gentle as a lamb, loud as a lion's roar and as delicate as glass yet tough as nails when crossed, done wrong and/or defending her babies/family and for these reasons and so many others we love our women. They're our rocks, our foundations, our friends, our sisters, mothers, aunts, grandmoms, our lovers and the base of our future. So love them, treat them with respect, loyalty, appreciation, dedication, commitment and most of all as you would treat yourself. Please my sons love the women in your life, provide, profess and protect them from all that would harm, hurt or do danger to them. They are to be loved not just sex items. Now it is not an easy task but it's possible. So be patient, be strong, be you and do godly things the benefits will be greatly. Now let the word of your mouth and the meditations of your heart be acceptable in the Creator's site and give you peace forever and ever. P.S. Pay attention!

Amen.

*L*OOKING INTO MY JOURNEY CALLED LIFE I'VE NOTICED that at times the lessons learned have mold me to see things a certain way. My start in life was modest. We had very little material things yet we have a lot of love and each other. Those two things have been the foundation of my world. I value the people in my circle. The presence of them makes life so beautiful. They have their own identities which makes the situation special; each one had a significant place and space in life. The thing I cherish the most about my childhood is the communication skills I learned from an early onset. It's what all are to be able to get along with others in society today. I feel that early communication with others is the key to some of the ills of society today. People lack the skills of communication today because of the advancement in technology which takes individuals away from each other. See there is nothing wrong with advancement cause it's change and change is constant in our lives. The issue that it promotes selfishness. It has taught them that they don't have to communicate with others directly and verbally which is the key for any community to be successful in society. See

I've learned that communication is the key to whatever a person intends to do in their life. Also communication is the main part of a community that's successful. If you look at communities when & where the communication levels are minimal at best there's sure to be violence, despair and poverty. This happens when the communication skills aren't there or they are at level of obscurity. I feel that if love and communication is part of your early childhood development it helps the community which makes society a better place. Developing communication skills is the start to whatever you choose to do in life it allows you to learn new things! Be able to get along with others. You learn problem solving skills. You learn how to listen to others' opinions and views. It opens your world to so much that you have endless choices. Communication allows you to decide right from wrong. Now I also understand that in today's society communication is mostly done via cell phones, Ipads, TV's and computers which is good for advancement in the technical aspect of life yet the presence of verbal relationships will always be a necessity. When two people speak to each other there is nothing in life that's more beautiful. The Creator made it this way that we must communicate with each other for the betterment of his creation. Think if we weren't made to communicate with each other then why did the creator make man and then woman so he wouldn't be alone. Also people pray which is communication with a person's deity. So communication is one of life's greatest gifts yet so many lack the knowledge and present of it. If you think I'm just saying this look around you today. The reason that some things are happening now is because of a lack of love and communication in the world. Social skills is something that most communities have issues with due to a ton of reasons but the most telling reason is the lack of verbally communicating with others. We need to remember that for a community to be strong and prosperous the communication amongst its members must be present. The social skills of society. It's biggest problem. I've also found that the problem is that people don't know how to communicate with each other. They talk reckless at each other instead of talking to each other. Again it starts with early development the ability to listen to another person, thoughts, opinions and views. So my sons don't be fast to judge, or be angry cause something said isn't what you agree on. Just remember the lessons taught to you. They will help you deal with whatever obstacles life places in your journey. Also remember that the lesson that you were afforded to receive isn't the same lessons others received. Always be humble and understanding to those less knowledgeable than self always using your communication & social skills to resolve any issue at hand. May the Creator bless you and keep you. May he lift up his face to shine and give you peace. May he be gracious to you and yours in whatsoever you chose to do.

Peace & Blessings

As I watch what's going on in society I have great concerns for my sons. I have watched you all become conditioned, fashioned, and programmed following the ways and customs of others. We have become generations of non-thinkers, non caring, stiff necked people. Funny thing about that is that the book used in all the courts, all the churches of different beliefs and most homes around the world states this yet most don't know that. It tells of all the trials and tribulations you will occur for being a follower of the ways and customs of others and forgetting who you are and the ways and customs of the Creator. See when you forget who you are you become whatever/whoever controls you which leads you to be conditioned, fashioned and programmed. Today most of society lives in this manner and it's what's called normal. Doing what the masses do is what is cool. That's what's called conditioned, fashioned and programmed. We are so far gone in these manners/actions that we don't even know ourselves. We don't know our history, our heritage, our language, our God. We have become generations of followers, gentiles, idol worshippers, slaves and by words. This is truly an unacceptable act in the eyes of the Creator. We have created and joined any and everything to be accepted and/or be part of an organization that doesn't want us in it nor is it about us in any shape, form or fashion. Again another coincidence this is the same manner that the creator presented his presence to Moses in the Mount no shape, form or fashion just a burning bush we are so programmed that we're fashioned and conditioned to forget this thru the religious overtones of the society we live in. The same people that enslaved us gave us deities to worship and of course the deity they gave us was made in his image. To control someone you first fashion their thought patterns; so to do this they gave us a god and convinced the slave that this god was better than their God and if they were caught serving another god other than the one they were given there would be consequences. Again this was an action taken from your spiritual book that the master used against you to control you due to your lack of knowledge of self. People are so programmed that the same things the Creator told us to do as a people we struggle to do or we don't do it at all yet we do whatever the slavemaster says to do like fearing him is more important than that of the Creator. We are so conditioned, fashioned and programmed that even thinking about the Sabbath (the Creator's day) is a rarity. We are taught to worship on the first day of the week yet the Creator says to rest on the seventh day and to argue the point the gentile is conditioned and programmed to say "That's when we were living under the law we are now living under grace". The sad thing is that being in the influence of the slave masters has caused generations of our people to continue being controlled, living in poverty, having lives of despair, being uneducated. This is far from what the creator intended for his chosen people to be. We are leaders, we are teachers. We are the truth. We keep the laws, the statues and commandments. We love

so think my sons don't allow yourself to be conditioned, fashioned or programmed. Now may the blessings of the creator be with you and keep you may he lift up his face to shine on you and give you peace.

Love
Your Father

14Nov16

TODAY I HAVE SUCH HEAVY THOUGHTS OF THE CONDITIONS of this country we live in and serve with the best of our abilities. I have lived through the civil rights movement, went to segregated schools until they decided to take the better students out of our schools and bus them to schools in other neighborhoods to enhance their GPA levels while the schools in our neighborhoods plummeted. This was part of the plan to keep our people in line, controlled, confused, disrespectful and most of all programmed. We have been so downtrodden, tyrannized, oppressed and repressed; to the blame of no one but ourselves. We as a people have failed each other because of the deep embedded self hatred we have as a people. This goes back to the covenant the Creator made with our ancestors at the mount. Yet we don't know this because of all the trials and tribulations that we have lived through and the disobedient ways and actions of our ancestors that are continually handed down from generations to generations. If this doesn't stop we will constantly be in a state of despair until we as a people become aware, wake up, see the "light" and realize we are the chosen people of the Creator.

Now I have read of others and heard about others' horror stories and how they were mistreated, abused and killed yet they are respected, well treated, ways and customs are honored and given national/worldly recognition. While the mentioning of what has happen to our people starts arguments of "why we can't let it go", "that was the past," "we gave you rights," "we acknowledge MLK day", "you have black history month". All excuses to not accept responsibility to what was done to us as a people and to continue to control, fashion and program us. Yet the issues didn't start there; they started with us being disobedient to the creator. We have forgotten our place, our history, our heritage, our culture cause we wanted and did what we wanted to instead of what was told of us to do by the creator we have tried to be like others, do like others, worship others deities, all in to be accepted by others instead of being self and being accepted by self and the creator. The actions of us not respecting each other has led to others not respecting us either. They can come from far lands, have different ways and customs yet when they come to this land they are taught to disrespect, not tolerate and to generally have total disregard for us as a people. Even to the tune that when they open businesses in our neighborhoods we protect them, serve them, work for them, call them mom & pop yet when/if one of our own does business in our neighborhood we don't patronize it, want favors and hookups, credit/shortages and don't pay the debt. Something that doesn't happen when we patronize others businesses. Why does this happen? It's cause of self hatred, being controlled, fashioned and programmed. Prime example just this past presidential election race the true colors of how we're viewed was shown by the candidate of the Republican Party Donald Trump who made racial sexual, rude bias statements towards people of color and those things were so overlooked that they and Donald Trump won the election and many of us cheered this, supported this and even said why not he can't do any worse than how we have been getting treated. Wow! How can they even think this way knowing the history of the person and his colleagues. Have we forgot about slavery, have we forgotten about civil rights, have we forgotten about segregation, have we forgotten about being whipped & hung, have we forgotten Tulsa, OK., have we forgotten about Rosewood, FL., have we forgotten MLK, Malcolm X, Meger Everetts and the multitude of others that have perished and continue to perish in these days with no change or consequences for these actions exhibited towards us. This will continue until we change our ways, our thoughts, our view of self, our relationships with the creator. Please my sons seek the creator and his love, truth, knowledge, ways, statues, laws, judgements and commandments. We will strive, be blessed, live in peace if we do what the creator told us to do. Which is to become the leaders we are, the light of the world, the salt of the earth and most of all his chosen people not servants of others. So may the creator bless you and keep you may he lift up his face to shine upon you. May he be gracious and give you peace. Strive to be the best you that YOU can be.

GN

28Nov16

I HAVE TO LET YOU KNOW THAT IN LIFE YOU WILL COME across all types of females and don't be so quick to explore the relations of a man and woman relationship. It is not as easy as it seems nor is it as hard as some make it. It starts with how your family structure is. Whether you have both parents or not you get your first relationship with a woman from your mother she will show you love, affection, treat you very special, tell you when you're wrong, adore you when you're right, show you how to survive yet you must remember she can only show you from a female perspective. She can not teach you love for a woman from how men view them cause she's a woman. We men see women differently we see women for what our needs are at the moment. Now we also must remember that all men learn differently how to love women based on how their relationships are with their own mothers and how they see their fathers, grandfathers, uncles treat their women again the first interaction that most males see with a woman is his father's relationship with his mother. Now the way your father interacts with your mother will be the foundation of your understanding of how to treat a woman. It is a gauge for you

33

to have to build a relationship with a woman yet not the only thing you will need. The relationship you build with the Creator will also be key to your relationship with a woman. She is a man's gift from the Creator so she must be adored, praised, loved and respected. She was made from man's rib for a reason cause the Creator knows the strength she bears. Seeing that the ribs are of great purpose to the body they support your structure hence the reason woman was made from the rib. They are located at your side and they hold up your body. This is the purpose of the woman to be strong, support and hold up her man. Now for this to happen, a male must first be a man yet many boys today like to commit acts of men yet not wanting/ knowing the responsibility that goes with these acts. A male should also understand what it means to wife a woman if he isn't ready for the responsibility of the act. See when you take a woman to wife it's the act that makes a marriage. This is an act before the creator after a male asked a father for his daughter. Nowadays this doesn't occur. Nowadays the customs of others have replaced the way the Creator made for us to be with a woman. See the Creator made all women with a "veil" on her vagina. With this veil this woman was called a virgin or maiden. This is not something that is of importance today, cause the purity of marriage is now based on the ceremony instead of that of a woman being a maiden for her husband. According to law the breaking of the maiden thru male penetration is true marriage. There are five types of women. A virgin - One that has not known a man, one who has never had sex and still has veil. A wife - One who submits her virginity or maiden to a man who becomes her husband. A concubine - One who openly sleeps with a man who has never admitted to anyone that he had taken her for a wife yet she continues to be a part of his sex life knowing he has a wife. A whore - this woman sleeps with any or every man she can. Some may say a whore is one who takes money for sexual services rendered. This is not true, yet there is a possibility that a whore can become a harlot. A harlot - this woman takes money for services rendered. So my sons don't be so hasty to rush into a situation with a woman without knowing and understanding the consequences of this relationship. You need to be patient, grow yourself, build character, set & achieve goals, build capital, get to know the Creator then maybe you will be ready for a true marriage. It's an honorable thing yet not respected in these days and times so if you choose to do things in this manner it is a step in the right direction and you can set a tone for those who follow you to do. Others may think that this is crazy yet if these values were taught and learned in our homes there would be less teenage pregnancies, unwed mothers and less disrespect towards women cause the person who carried you 9 months and brought you into this world is a woman. So love them, cherish them, appreciate them and constantly show them true love and respect at any cost. Tell them what they truly mean to you cause your daughters are watching and how you want them to be treated should always be on your mind. Peace and blessings.

GN

10Dec16

*H*EY MY SONS I WANT TO PASS ON TO YOU THE ART OF reading books. Especially those of substance. Meaning read books of self, books of growth emotionally, physically and financially. Books of history (of self, as well as others) books of education, books of spiritual growing. This is the reason I wrote these letters for you to enhance your reading skills and to give you a part of me no one could give to you except a father, a teacher, a leader, a man, a child of the Creator so I'm ending these letters with a few poems that may give you some insight on life itself as well as getting to know another side of your father. So may the Creator keep you and lift up his countenance to shine on you and give you peace. I bless you all, Amen....

Your Father
Love Always & Forever

"Don't Call Me Brother"

Don't call me brother
And take the last coat that I've got
How the hell am I your brother
And you're stabbing me in the back
Don't call me brother
While you're holding a gun to my head
What kind of a brother are you
Wanting me dead
Don't call me brother
And don't give a damn about me
How can we be brothers
When you can't even recognize me
Don't call me brother
When you're way over there
We can never be brothers
Cause I'm cold and lonely down here
Don't call me brother
When you don't know my mommy
You are not my brother
You killed my daddy
Don't call me brother
When your big boots walk on my toe
Brothers feel the pain
Of theirs brothers in the ghetto
Don't call me brother
When it don't mean a thing
You've moved out of town
Cause you made it big
Don't call me brother
When you're making millions
A big brother would care

About the little ones
Don't call me brother
Raising your fist up high
Cause you never saw tears
Coming from my eye
Don't call me brother
Cause you only look like me
We lost that bond
Long after slavery
Now you're calling me brother
Oh why can't you see
We are not brothers
Cause we're not a family
You have another father
And I retain our old dad
So please don't call me brother
The whole situation is so sad

"W-O-M-A-N"

She's my mother - my father's wife
She's the one who gave me life
She's my sister - she's my friend
A relationship that can never end
She's my daughter - oh! she's my child
Who'll be a mother all over again

The symbol of creation - that's my wife
The strength of the other half of my life
She moulds the seed - just like the land
She gave birth to every man

She's beautiful - she's precious
She's great and marvelous
Without her would mean
Without me
Without her there is no man
She's the source of all
She's woman
She's woman.

"Who Is An Israelite?"

It would be to sleep and not to die
Cause you are of the truth, not of the lie
And when your name is called in the book of life
You'll say Thank God Almighty I'm an Israelite